Finding a HOME

Story by **Julie Lane**

Pictures by **Pilar P. Luna**

AuthorHouse™
1663 Liberty Drive
Bloomington, IN 47403
www.authorhouse.com
Phone: 833-262-8899

This book is printed on acid-free paper.

ISBN: 978-1-6655-4774-1 (sc)
ISBN: 978-1-6655-4773-4 (e)

Library of Congress Control Number: 2021925659

Print information available on the last page.

Published by AuthorHouse 12/23/2021

authorHOUSE®

**This story is told with love to honor
all of Julie and Rick's pets. JL**

On a cold November morning, a little brown, furry puppy is seen running through the neighborhood.

Where do you come from, Puppy?

Sitting on the front porch of one house in the neighborhood, a bright orange pumpkin grabs the puppy's attention. Playing with the pumpkin, the puppy seems to feel safe.

After a few minutes, she curls up on that porch, quickly falling asleep!

Are you tired, Puppy?

Someone is watching. Inside the house, a man is unsure of what to do when he spies the sleeping puppy. He texts his wife, asking for advice. She does not reply!

Later, the man is working in his backyard when he looks up to see the little brown, furry puppy sitting on his back porch. She has chosen his house!

Do you need a home, Puppy?

The man scoops up the puppy and sees no collar; she likes the cozy warmth of his arms. He crosses the street to consult with a neighbor who loves dogs, and, using their phones, they try to find the puppy's owner.

Hoping to hear from someone, the man returns to his house with the furry puppy who is now snuggling in his arms. The man's wife calls on the phone, asking, "What is happening?"

Are you safe, Puppy?

In the warm kitchen, the man explains that the puppy is with him in their house; he is hoping to hear from an owner.

Soon, the wife joins the man and puppy as the people watch her play and sleep on the kitchen rug.

What happens now, Puppy?

Soon the couple travels with the puppy to a local veterinarian, asking those who work there to see if the puppy has a chip inserted under her skin. No chip exists!

ARIAN

Everyone who works at the vet clinic wants to pet and hold the puppy–she is SO soft! Her brindle coat is SO pretty!

Everyone loves you, Puppy!

After four days of searching for an owner of the puppy, the couple decides to keep her!

They visit their own vet who inserts an ID chip, gives the necessary shots, weighs her (12 pounds), estimates her age (10-12 weeks), and discusses plans for making a new home for the puppy.

Is this your new family, Puppy?

Now, this puppy needs a name! The man and his wife ask their five granddaughters to help them choose a name. After receiving MANY excellent choices, they decide to call the puppy Cocoa; the name suits her brindle coat and four white paws.

Now the three of them really are a family!

Welcome home, Cocoa!

Soon, Cocoa meets her extended family. All the granddaughters love her! She meets two of the girls in person and three more via Skype; several months later, Cocoa travels to Oregon to meet those three in person.

The family dogs—Sarah, Teddy, and Truman—are hesitant about Cocoa's playfulness but finally are ready to accept her!

SARAH

TRUMAN

TEDDY

Welcome to the family, Cocoa!

Winter arrives, bringing unique experiences for Cocoa. She quickly learns that snow is exciting, cold, and wet!

She loves to eat clumps of snow, dig into piles of snow, and chase the flying snowflakes!

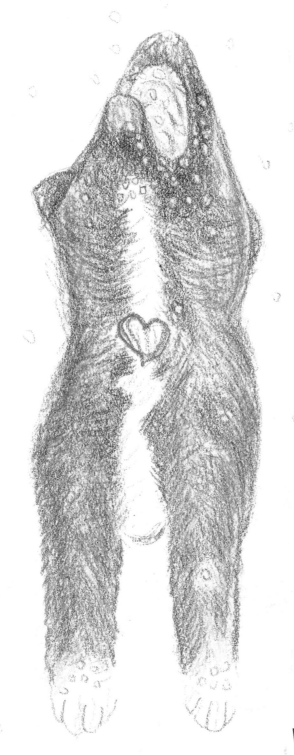

What fun, Cocoa!

Cocoa makes lots of friends in the neighborhood!

Birdie and Cocoa share backyards together, becoming best friends!

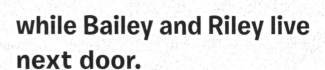

Sadie lives across the backyard,

while Bailey and Riley live next door.

Max lives across the street.

Thor, Jane, and Zelda
live down the street.

Welcome to the neighborhood, Cocoa!

HOLLY

BONNIE

HARPER

WINSTON

FINLEY

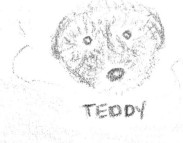

TEDDY

OTIS & SHUG

Lots of dogs meet
Cocoa on walks
each day!

Cocoa is a puppy and always wants to play. Some of her doggie friends are waiting for her to grow up so she will stop jumping so much!

LEIA

GRACIE

KIKI

LILY

ROSIE

BREWSTER

Welcome to a new dog pack, Cocoa!

Many neighborhood people love Cocoa! She makes friends on her daily walks—some children, some adults, some senior citizens. Everyone wants to feel her soft fur; a few let her lick their faces; others like to watch her grow up, commenting on how big she is becoming!

Once in a while, someone opens a front door, coming out of the house to ask about her; occasionally children come to the door of her house, asking if Cocoa can play!

Your neighborhood is filled with friends, Cocoa!

Cocoa enjoys traveling in the car–to the pet store for food, to the hiking trails for walks, to homes of her extended family for visits! Feeling the breeze on her face is terrific as she looks out the back window. A really great drive means she gets to ride in the front seat next to her favorite driver!

Your world is large, Cocoa!

Cocoa is over one year old now! She weighs 50 pounds and loves to run–fast! She chases squirrels, lounges in the cool green grass, and wanders around the backyard of the house she chose many months earlier.

Finding a home was her goal as a puppy long ago. Now she has a family, friends, AND a home!

What a happy dog you are, Cocoa!

ABOUT THE AUTHOR–

As a mother, grandmother, and community college English teacher, Julie Lane loves to share stories! She has already published *Welcome, Baby Owls!* In the fall of 2019, when Cocoa chooses to live with her and her husband, Rick, Julie knows she has another story to tell! She hopes the excitement, experienced by her granddaughters and all the children in the neighborhood when Cocoa arrived, spills onto the pages of this book!

ABOUT THE ILLUSTRATOR–

Pilar P. Luna is a freelance designer in the Kansas City area. Her family originated from Lima, Peru, and immigrated here in 1964. Born in Kansas City, she now lives in Overland Park, Kansas. This is the second children's book Julie and Pilar have created together; *Welcome, Baby Owls!* was published in 2007. Pilar has also written and illustrated another book for children-- *Hello, Sunny Day!*